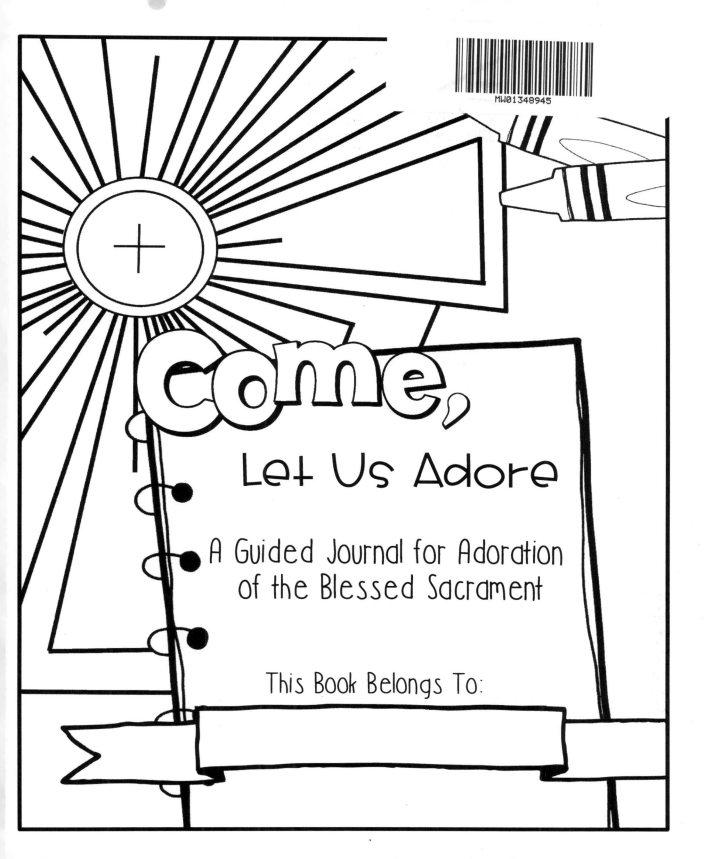

Copyright © 2018 Jennifer Sharpe

All rights reserved. No part of this publication may be reproduced, distributed, or transmitted in any form or by any means, including photocopying, recording, or other electronic or mechanical means, without the prior written permission of the publisher. Reviewers have permission to use brief passages and images from the book for review purposes only.

ISBN-13: 978-1721776726

ISBN-10: 1721776729

Clip art:

@Dancing Crayons Designs
http://www.teacherspayteachers.com/Store/Dancing-Crayons-Designs
@The Clipart Factory
http:/www.teacherspayteachers.com/Store/The-Clipart-Factory
@Loving Lit
http://www.teacherspayteachers.com/Store/Lovin-Lit
@Trioriginals
http://www.teacherspayteachers.com/Store/Trioriginals
@Jennifer Sharpe
www.fb.me/jennifersharpe.author

Fonts:

@Kaitliynn Albani
https://www.teacherspayteachers.com/Product/KA-Fonts-Complete-Font-Bundle-Growing-Bundle-2828325

Scripture texts in this work are taken from the New American Bible, revised edition © 2010, 1991, 1986, 1970 Confraternity of Christian Doctrine, Washington, D.C. and are used by permission of the copyright owner. All Rights Reserved. No part of the New American Bible may be reproduced in any form without permission in writing from the copyright owner.

Every reasonable effort has been made to determine copyright holders of excerpted materials, fonts, and graphics and to secure permissions as needed. If any copyrighted materials have been inadvertently used without proper credit being given, please contact Jennifer Sharpe in writing so that future editions may be corrected.

Book Design by Jennifer Sharpe

Published by Jennifer Sharpe

Contact:
jennifersharpe.author@gmail.com
fb.me/jennifersharpe.author

Keep in Touch!

Like my Book?

Leave an Amazon review! It only takes a moment, and it really helps!

I love hearing your feedback!

Have a question? Want to review my book on your blog or website? Feel free to contact me by email any time!

Email:
jennifersharpe.author@gmail.com

New books are coming out all the time! Follow me on Facebook, Amazon, or Instagram for giveaways, discounts, book walk-through videos, and updates on my work:

Facebook Author Page:
fb.me/jennifersharpe.author

Amazon Author Page:
amazon.com/author/jennifersharpe

Instagram:
www.instagram.com/jennifersharpe.author

Help your children fall in love with the Mass. Try my other books:

My First Interactive Mass Book for Catholic Kids, an interactive guide to the Catholic Mass, for ages 3 to 7

The Mass Book for Catholic Children, a guided Mass journal for ages 7 to 12

Available on Amazon.com and other online retailers.

For the Parent

Our children live in a world that is constantly going, going, going. Between school commitments, extracurricular activities, sports, music lessons, dance classes, and a myriad of other things, it may seem that there is simply no time to take your child to Adoration of the Blessed Sacrament. To think this way is a serious mistake. If you want your child to remain a faithful Catholic when they are grown, you must help them to fall in love with Our Lord, who is really and truly present in the Eucharist. They must recognize that they worship a God who is present to them in a very real way in the Blessed Sacrament, just because he loves them so much and wants very badly to spend time with them. Aside from the Holy Sacrifice of the Mass, Adoration is the chief way that we can help our children recognize the enduring love of Jesus for them. Spending time with Jesus in the Eucharist is truly crucial to their spiritual health and well-being. Now is the time to start taking your child to Adoration. Start with short visits (10 or 15 minutes at a time), once or twice a month, and work your way up to longer visits of 30 minutes or more each week.

You may be met with resistance or outright refusal when you invite your children to join you in Adoration of the Blessed Sacrament. Typically when a child is reticent to visit Jesus in the Eucharist it is because he or she really doesn't understand what they are actually being invited to do – that is, to spend time with the One who created the earth, who died for their sins, and who is humbly waiting every moment to visit with them. *Come, Let Us Adore* will help make this message plain to them, and gently encourage them to give Adoration a try.

Come, Let Us Adore was created to help your child learn to love spending time with Jesus in Adoration. In it you will find page after page of meaningful activities that will help your child learn to quiet their mind and heart before Jesus in the Eucharist. Included in this book are twenty 4-page spreads. One 4-page spread may be used per visit, or, if your visits are very short, split up over two or more visits to Adoration. *Come, Let Us Adore* contains both repeating activities, such as structured prayer prompts and time spent each visit simply gazing quietly at Jesus exposed in the monstrance, and non-repeating activities, such as looking up a different Scripture passage at each visit or drawing a Holy Card based on an assigned Rosary

For the Parent

mystery. All the activities are worthwhile, and will encourage your child, in a really fun and gentle way, to draw, write, and color as they share whatever is on their hearts with Our Lord. Other activities include: practicing both spontaneous and memorized prayer, pondering (and coloring!) a new name for Jesus and recording what it means to them, meditating on a new mystery of the Rosary at each visit, and answering open ended questions that are designed to help the child grow closer to Jesus through honest communication with him in prayer.

Before you give the book to your child, take a minute to go over the instructional pages at the front of the book with them, making sure they understand how to complete each activity, how to use the appendix at the back, and how to find a passage in the Bible. The passages cited in this book come from the New American Bible, Revised Edition (NABRE). This will only take a few minutes, and will really raise the quality of interaction your child has with the book. In addtion, I recommend providing your child with crayons or colored pencils for use with this book (markers will bleed through the pages).

As your child uses the book, it is highly likely that they will come to you with questions about their faith. Don't be afraid of these questions, for questions are a sign that your child is curious about their faith and would like to learn more – and that's a good thing! If you find that you don't have the answers, don't panic! Learn together. Take them to the Catholic bookstore for some new reading material. Listen to a Catholic podcast together. Open up the Catechism or your Bible with your child, or speak with your parish priest. The more you show your willingness to learn, the more your child will too.

May the Lord bless you in your efforts as you raise your child to love Jesus in the Eucharist. I pray that this book will be a useful tool that you can rely on to help your child learn to love spending time with Our Lord, truly present to them in the Blessed Sacrament.

For the Child

Do you realize that you have an extraordinary gift in your Catholic faith? Do you know what it is? I'll tell you. Every day, in parishes all over the world, God comes to visit with his people; indeed he visits with us in the most special way possible during Holy Communion. This is what we call the Holy Sacrifice of the Mass. In the Mass, Our Lord, Jesus Christ, makes himself present in the Eucharist so that he can be with us in the most intimate way possible. Jesus is truly present in the Host — Body, Blood, Soul, and Divinity. This is his gift to us.

But there's something even more extraordinary that I think you ought to know too. As a Catholic, you probably have learned that Jesus is God, and that he came to earth as a man, and suffered and died so that all people would have the opportunity of friendship with him in Heaven. But do you realize that even if you were the only person on earth, Jesus would still have come? He would still have come because he loves YOU. Jesus loves *everybody*, yes. But he loves every person as an *individual*, and he is interested in every small thing that happens to you, both the good and the bad. The bottom line is this: Jesus loves YOU and he wants very much to spend time with you whenever you are able.

Because Jesus loves you that much, he has made himself available to you through prayer all of the time. You can pray anywhere and at any time, and Jesus will be there to listen. But he has also made himself available to you in a very real and special way in Adoration of the Blessed Sacrament. Adoration of the Blessed Sacrament is when one of the consecrated Hosts from a previous Mass is placed into a monstrance (a golden stand with a circular window that holds the Host). The monstrance is placed high so that all can see Jesus in the Eucharist when they come to the church to pray.

There is something very special about sharing your heart with Jesus in Adoration. Seeing him high in the monstrance, just quietly waiting for you to spend time with him should make you feel very loved and cherished by God. But prayer takes practice, and if you haven't spent much time talking with Jesus, then going to visit him in Adoration can be tough. This book will help you with that.

For the Child

In this book you will find many meaningful and fun things to do that will help you learn to feel comfortable spending time talking to Jesus. You will learn a new name for Jesus every time you visit him in Adoration. You will learn to look up verses in your Bible and spend time thinking about what the words mean to you. You will pray a decade of the Rosary at each visit, coloring in the beads on the page as you go. You will draw your own Holy Card showing an event from Our Lord's life. Most importantly, you will learn to be still and quiet with Jesus in the Eucharist. You will be given many opportunities to share with him anything you want to share – both the good and the bad things, for he wants to hear everything that you want to tell him, and he is always there, ready to listen.

Take a moment to flip through the book now and get a feel for the kinds of activities that are included. The first 4 pages show you in detail how to complete each activity and give helpful tips for using the book, so be sure to check those out! There is also an appendix at the back that lists all of the books of the Bible, all of the mysteries of the Rosary, and all of the basic prayers of the Rosary, just in case you need to look at those as you do some of the activities. You can also use the Reconciliation Record Sheet at the back of the book to keep track of when you go to Confession.

I pray that as you use this book, you will learn to open up your heart to Jesus – your God, truly present to you in the Blessed Sacrament.

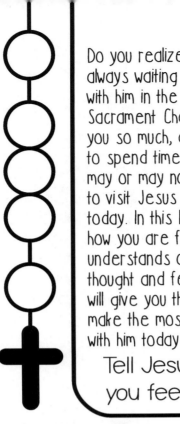

Do you realize that Jesus is always waiting for you to visit with him in the Blessed Sacrament Chapel? He loves you so much, and can't wait to spend time with you. You may or may not be excited to visit Jesus in Adoration today. In this box, tell Jesus how you are feeling. He understands our every thought and feeling, and he will give you the grace to make the most of your visit with him today.

Tell Jesus how you feel today.

Date: Write the date here.

Time in: What time did you arrive?

Time out: What time did you leave?

Spend time gazing upon Jesus.

Our Catholic Faith teaches us that Jesus is really and truly present in the Blessed Sacrament. This is truly a precious gift to us as Catholics because it means that wherever there are consecrated Hosts, Our Lord is really present there just waiting to spend time with us. Whenever you see the Tabernacle, kneel down and thank Jesus for always being there to spend time with you. For this activity, spend some time (5 to 10 minutes would be good) just gazing at the Host. Then write any words that come to mind in the box.

Use the rosary beads to pray the beginning of the rosary. Color each bead as you pray. If you need help with the prayers, see the back of this book!

What words come to mind? Write them here.

Each letter of the word P.R.A.Y. stands for a different kind of prayer. Use the boxes below to pray each kind of prayer.

Praise – What are you thankful for?

It can be easy to take for granted all the things we have to be thankful for. Here is a chance to let Jesus know that you appreciate all the wonderful gifts and blessings he has given to you.

Repent – What are you sorry for?

Sin not only hurts our relationship with Jesus; it also hurts our relationships with other people. In this box you may confess some of the poor choices you have made lately, and ask for the grace to do better next time.

Ask – What is something you would like to ask God for?

Everyone has something they would like to ask God for. Like any good Father, God wants to give us good things that will help us on our journey to Heaven. Write down your special intentions here.

Yield – What is something that you worry about? Give it to God.

Jesus cares about everything you care about. If you are worried about something, here is a chance to tell Jesus all about it, and to ask him to give you the grace to trust him with your worries and fears.

The Luminous Mysteries – The Institution of the Eucharist at the Last Supper

Read John 6:35 – 51
Words I Liked

Every time you come to Adoration you will focus on a different name for Jesus. This name will be loosely tied to the rosary mystery that you will be praying, and will usually appear in the Scripture verse listed above. Look up the verse in your Bible. On the lines provided, write a few of your favorite words or phrases from the verses.

Every time you visit Adoration, you can say one decade of the rosary (you may color the beads on the left side of the page as you pray). To the left of the rosary beads you can see which mystery to think about while you are praying. When you finish this book you will have meditated on every mystery at least once! Draw a picture depicting the mystery in this box, or if you already have a holy card for this mystery, you may tape it here instead!

Last Supper Holy Card

Bread of Life

A different name for Jesus will appear in fancy lettering at the top of this box each time you come to Adoration. You may think about what this name means to you as you color each letter. Then, on the lines provided, spend a little time answering the question at the bottom of this box. Hint: Reading the assigned passage for the day will help you answer the question, but keep in mind that there are no set answers to these questions. The goal of this activity is to help you to think about who Jesus is.

At the Last Supper, Jesus gave us his flesh to eat. In the passage, he says that he is the Bread of Life. What does it mean to say that Jesus is the Bread of Life?

Write one thing you love about Jesus.
This page will be the same each time, though your answers may be different! Take a little time to think about each question on this page before you answer it. In this box, tell Jesus one thing you love about him.

Write one reason why you are glad you came here.
Even if you were reluctant to come to Adoration today, I bet there are some reasons you are glad you came anyway. In this box, tell Jesus one reason you are glad that you visited him in Adoration today.

What is one thing you can thank Jesus for today?
You may not often think about all the little gifts and blessings that Jesus gives to you each day. Take a moment now to thank him for his gifts to you. Be specific.

You may say anything you want to Jesus in this box. He loves you no matter what you say or how you feel.

What is one thing you would like to say to Jesus today?

Each letter of the word P.R.A.Y. stands for a different kind of prayer. Use the boxes below to pray each kind of prayer.

Praise – What are you thankful for?

Repent – What are you sorry for?

Ask – What is something you would like to ask God for?

Yield – What is something that you worry about? Give it to God.

Read Psalm 63:5 – 9
Words I Liked

_____
_____
_____
_____
_____
_____
_____

Annunciation Holy Card

The Joyful Mysteries – The Annunciation of Gabriel to the Virgin Mary

Savior

_____
_____
_____
_____

What does it mean to say that Jesus is our Savior?

Write one thing you love about Jesus.

Write one reason why you are glad you came here.

What is one thing you can thank Jesus for today?

Thank You, Jesus.

What is one thing you would like to say to Jesus today?

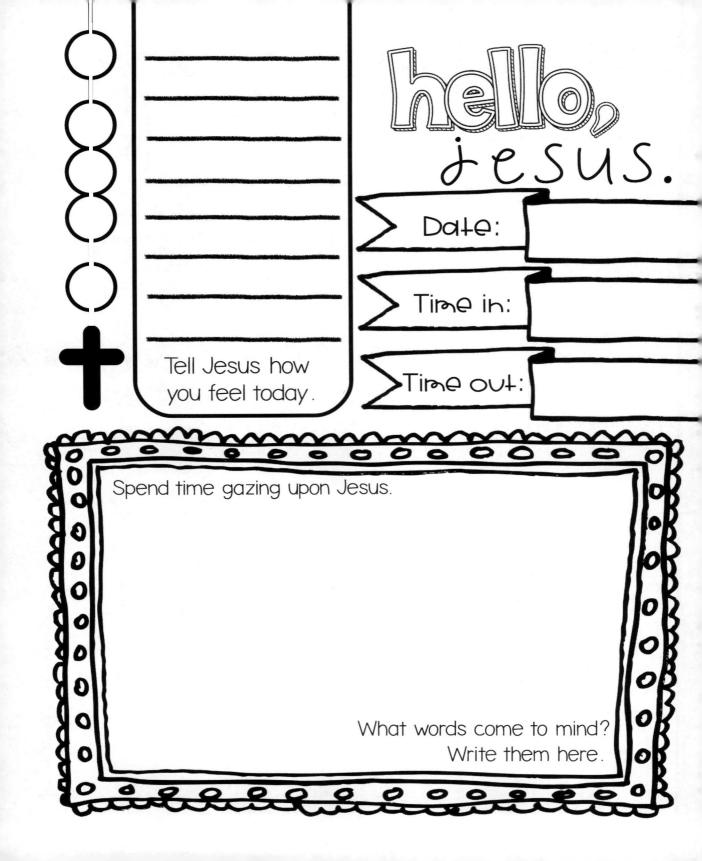

Each letter of the word P.R.A.Y. stands for a different kind of prayer. Use the boxes below to pray each kind of prayer.

 Praise – What are you thankful for?

 Repent – What are you sorry for?

 Ask – What is something you would like to ask God for?

 Yield – What is something that you worry about? Give it to God.

Read Luke 1:39 – 45
Words I Liked

_____
_____
_____
_____
_____
_____
_____

Visitation Holy Card

Lord

_____
_____
_____
_____

At the visitation, Elizabeth says that Jesus is her Lord. What does she mean by that?

The Joyful Mysteries – The Visitation of the Virgin Mary to Elizabeth

Each letter of the word P.R.A.Y. stands for a different kind of prayer. Use the boxes below to pray each kind of prayer.

Praise — What are you thankful for?

Repent — What are you sorry for?

Ask — What is something you would like to ask God for?

Yield — What is something that you worry about? Give it to God.

Read Matthew 1:18 – 23
Words I Liked

_____
_____
_____
_____
_____
_____
_____

Nativity Holy Card

Emmanuel

Emmanuel means "God with Us".

_____
_____
_____
_____

What does it mean to say that Jesus is "God with Us"? How does that make you feel?

The Joyful Mysteries – The Birth of Jesus

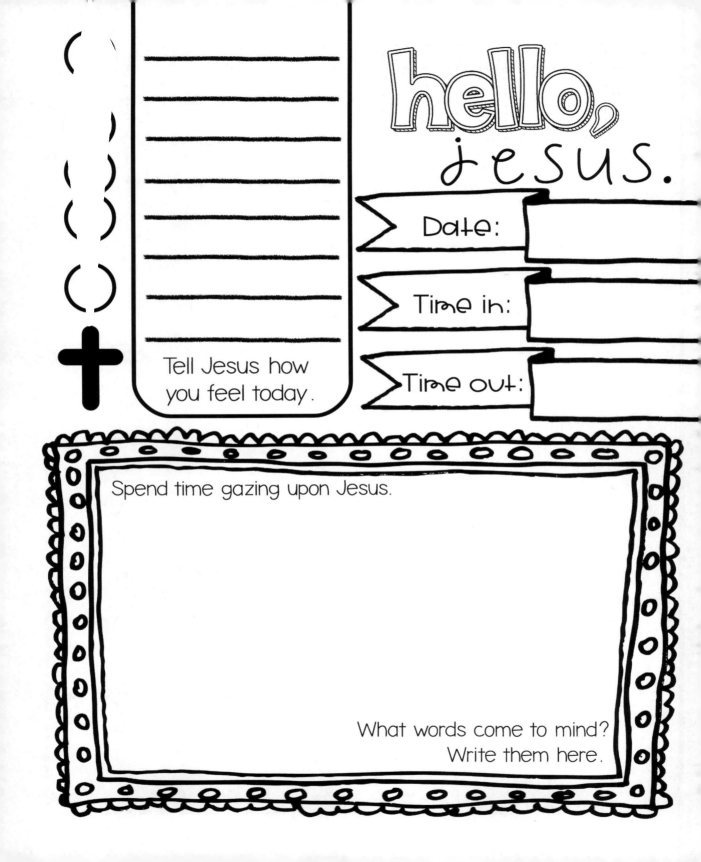

Each letter of the word P.R.A.Y. stands for a different kind of prayer. Use the boxes below to pray each kind of prayer.

Praise – What are you thankful for?

Ask – What is something you would like to ask God for?

Yield – What is something that you worry about? Give it to God.

Read Luke 2:22 – 32
Words I Liked

Presentation Holy Card

Messiah

Messiah means "chosen one".

What does it mean to say that Jesus is the Messiah? What was he chosen for?

The Joyful Mysteries – The Presentation of Jesus in the Temple

Each letter of the word P.R.A.Y. stands for a different kind of prayer. Use the boxes below to pray each kind of prayer.

Praise – What are you thankful for?

Repent – What are you sorry for?

Ask – What is something you would like to ask God for?

Yield – What is something that you worry about? Give it to God.

The Joyful Mysteries – The Finding of the Child Jesus at the Temple

Read John 14:1 – 10
Words I Liked
_____
_____
_____
_____
_____
_____
_____

Finding Jesus at the Temple Holy Card

the Truth

_____
_____
_____
_____

The Bible says that everyone who heard Jesus was amazed by his answers. In the passage, Jesus says that he is the Truth. What does it mean to say that Jesus is the Truth?

Write one thing you love about Jesus.

Write one reason why you are glad you came here.

What is one thing you can thank Jesus for today?

Thank You, Jesus.

What is one thing you would like to say to Jesus today?

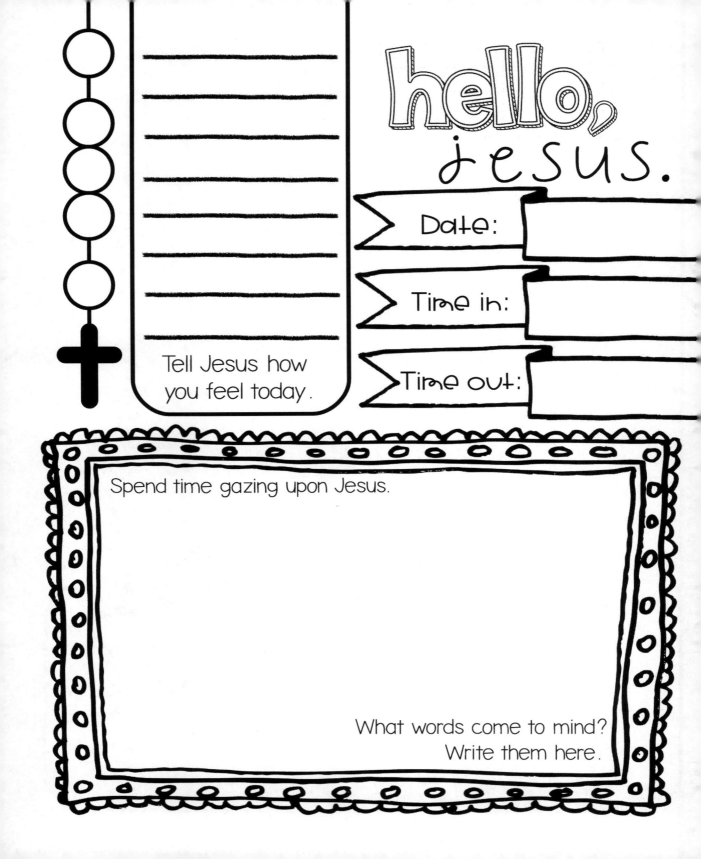

Each letter of the word P.R.A.Y. stands for a different kind of prayer. Use the boxes below to pray each kind of prayer.

 Praise – What are you thankful for?

 Repent – What are you sorry for?

 Ask – What is something you would like to ask God for?

 Yield – What is something that you worry about? Give it to God.

The Luminous Mysteries – The Baptism of Jesus in the Jordan River

Read Matthew 16:13 – 17
Words I Liked
_____
_____
_____
_____
_____
_____
_____

Baptism of Jesus
Holy Card

Son of God

_____
_____
_____
_____

At Jesus' baptism, the Father says that Jesus is his Beloved Son. In the passage, Peter says the same thing. What does it mean to say that Jesus is the Son of God?

Write one thing you love about Jesus.

Write one reason why you are glad you came here.

What is one thing you can thank Jesus for today?

Thank You, Jesus.

What is one thing you would like to say to Jesus today?

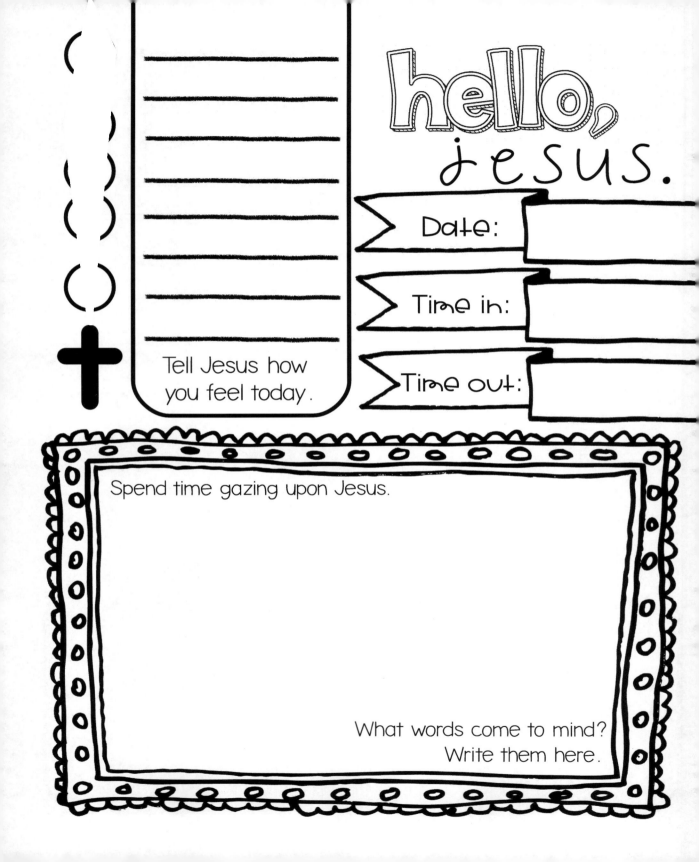

Each letter of the word P.R.A.Y. stands for a different kind of prayer. Use the boxes below to pray each kind of prayer.

Praise – What are you thankful for?

Repent – What are you sorry for?

Ask – What is something you would like to ask God for?

Yield – What is something that you worry about? Give it to God.

Read John 4:7 – 42
Words I Liked

Wedding at Cana Holy Card

LIVING water

At Cana, Jesus turned water into wine. In the passage you read, Jesus talks about Living Water.
What is the Living Water that Jesus gives us?

The Luminous Mysteries – The Wedding Feast at Cana

Each letter of the word P.R.A.Y. stands for a different kind of prayer. Use the boxes below to pray each kind of prayer.

Praise – What are you thankful for?

Repent – What are you sorry for?

Ask – What is something you would like to ask God for?

Yield – What is something that you worry about? Give it to God.

The Luminous Mysteries – The Proclamation of the Kingdom of Heaven

Read John 1:10 – 18
Words I Liked
_____
_____
_____
_____
_____
_____
_____

Jesus Proclaims
the Kingdom
Holy Card

the WORD

_____
_____
_____
_____

The passage says that,
"the Word became flesh and made his dwelling among us."
What does it mean to say that Jesus is the Word?

Each letter of the word P.R.A.Y. stands for a different kind of prayer. Use the boxes below to pray each kind of prayer.

Praise – What are you thankful for?

Repent – What are you sorry for?

Ask – What is something you would like to ask God for?

Yield – What is something that you worry about? Give it to God.

The Luminous Mysteries – The Transfiguration of Jesus

Read John 8:12
Words I Liked

Transfiguration Holy Card

LIGHT of the WORLD

In the Transfiguration, Jesus shines with light.
In the passage, Jesus says that he is the Light of the World.
What does that mean?

Write one thing you love about Jesus.

Write one reason why you are glad you came here.

What is one thing you can thank Jesus for today?

Thank You, Jesus.

What is one thing you would like to say to Jesus today?

Each letter of the word P.R.A.Y. stands for a different kind of prayer. Use the boxes below to pray each kind of prayer.

Praise – What are you thankful for?

Repent – What are you sorry for?

Ask – What is something you would like to ask God for?

Yield – What is something that you worry about? Give it to God.

The Luminous Mysteries – The Institution of the Eucharist at the Last Supper

Read John 6:35 – 51
Words I Liked

_____
_____
_____
_____
_____
_____

Last Supper
Holy Card

Bread of Life

_____
_____
_____
_____

At the Last Supper, Jesus gave us his flesh to eat. In the passage, he says that he is the Bread of Life. What does it mean to say that Jesus is the Bread of Life?

Each letter of the word P.R.A.Y. stands for a different kind of prayer. Use the boxes below to pray each kind of prayer.

Praise — What are you thankful for?

Repent — What are you sorry for?

Ask — What is something you would like to ask God for?

Yield — What is something that you worry about? Give it to God.

Read John 10:11 – 15
Words I Liked

_____
_____
_____
_____
_____
_____

The Agony in the Garden Holy Card

GOOD SHEPHERD

_____
_____
_____
_____

The passages says that, "a good shepherd lays down his life for the sheep." What does it mean to say that Jesus is our Good Shepherd?

The Sorrowful Mysteries – The Agony of Jesus in the Garden

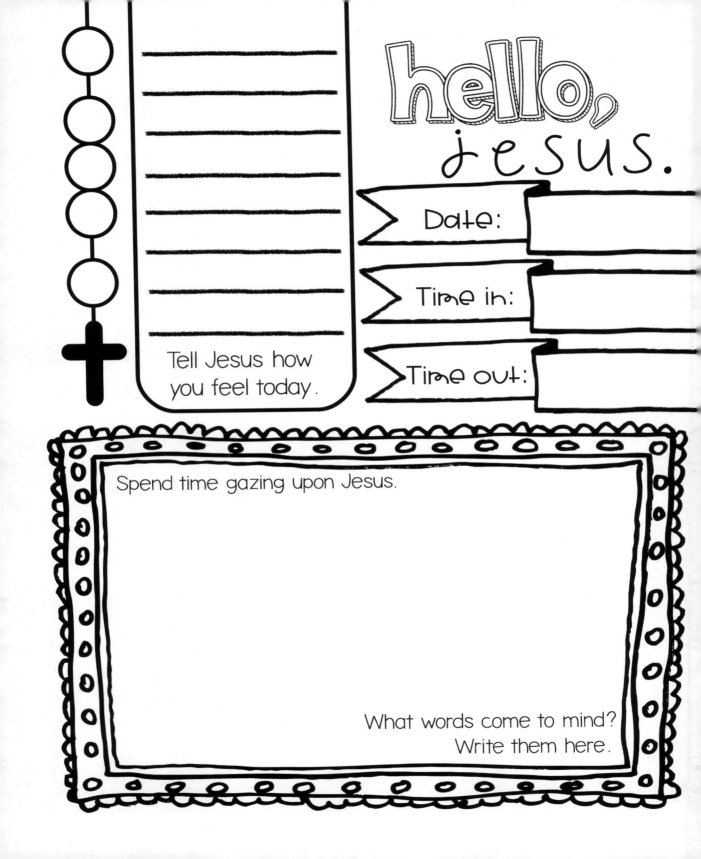

Each letter of the word P.R.A.Y. stands for a different kind of prayer. Use the boxes below to pray each kind of prayer.

Praise – What are you thankful for?

Repent – What are you sorry for?

Ask – What is something you would like to ask God for?

Yield – What is something that you worry about? Give it to God.

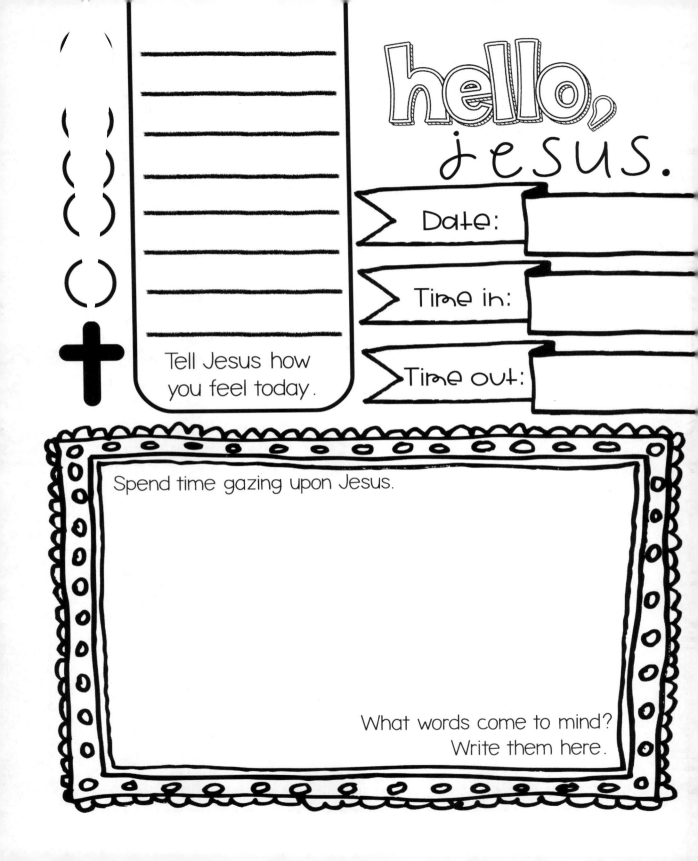

Each letter of the word P.R.A.Y. stands for a different kind of prayer. Use the boxes below to pray each kind of prayer.

 Praise – What are you thankful for?

 Repent – What are you sorry for?

 Ask – What is something you would like to ask God for?

 Yield – What is something that you worry about? Give it to God.

Read Revelation 17:14
Words I Liked

_____
_____
_____
_____
_____
_____
_____

Crowning with Thorns Holy Card

The Sorrowful Mysteries – Jesus is Crowned with Thorns

King

_____
_____
_____
_____

The soldiers mocked Jesus with a crown of thorns, but according to the passage Jesus really is our King. What does that mean to you?

Write one thing you love about Jesus.

Write one reason why you are glad you came here.

What is one thing you can thank Jesus for today?

Thank You, Jesus.

What is one thing you would like to say to Jesus today?

Each letter of the word P.R.A.Y. stands for a different kind of prayer. Use the boxes below to pray each kind of prayer.

Praise – What are you thankful for?

Repent – What are you sorry for?

Ask – What is something you would like to ask God for?

Yield – What is something that you worry about? Give it to God.

Read Matthew 16:24 – 27
Words I Liked

Jesus Carries his Cross Holy Card

the WAY

In the passage, Jesus tells us that we must take up our crosses and follow him. He is the Way.
What does it mean for you to follow the Way?

The Sorrowful Mysteries – Jesus Carries the Cross to Calvary

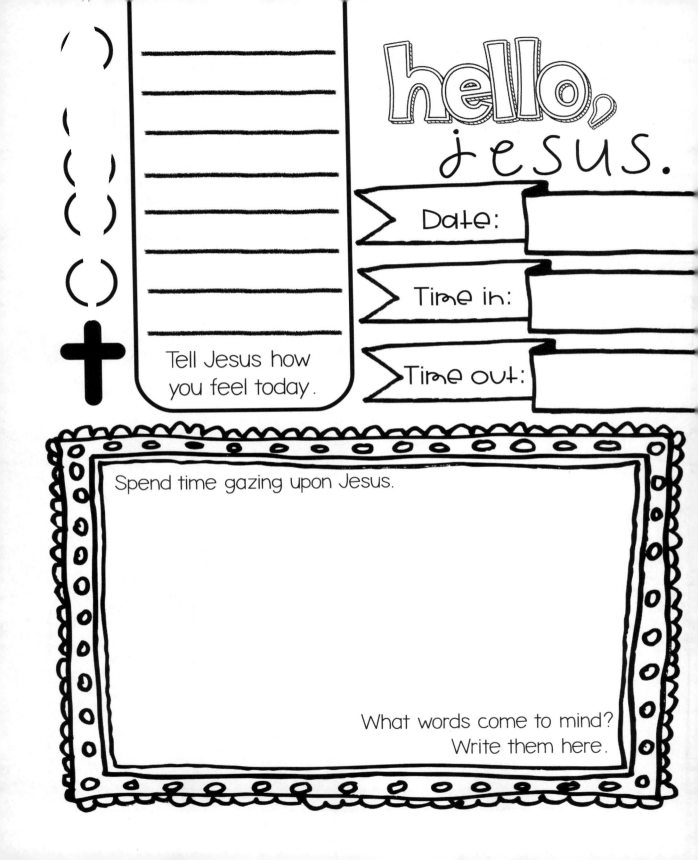

Each letter of the word P.R.A.Y. stands for a different kind of prayer. Use the boxes below to pray each kind of prayer.

Praise – What are you thankful for?

Repent – What are you sorry for?

Ask – What is something you would like to ask God for?

Yield – What is something that you worry about? Give it to God.

The Sorrowful Mysteries – The Crucifixion of Jesus

Read Exodus 12:21 – 23
Words I Liked

_____
_____
_____
_____
_____
_____
_____

Crucifixion Holy Card

Lamb of God

_____
_____
_____
_____

In the passage, the Israelites must put the blood of a perfect lamb on their doorposts to be saved. In the New Testament, John the Baptist calls Jesus the Lamb of God.
How is Jesus the Lamb of God?

Each letter of the word P.R.A.Y. stands for a different kind of prayer. Use the boxes below to pray each kind of prayer.

Praise – What are you thankful for?

Repent – What are you sorry for?

Ask – What is something you would like to ask God for?

Yield – What is something that you worry about? Give it to God.

Read John 11:25 – 27
Words I Liked

_____
_____
_____
_____
_____
_____
_____

Resurrection Holy Card

Resurrection

To resurrect means to restore to life.

_____
_____
_____
_____

What does it mean to say that Jesus is the Resurrection?

The Glorious Mysteries – The Resurrection of Jesus

Each letter of the word P.R.A.Y. stands for a different kind of prayer. Use the boxes below to pray each kind of prayer.

Praise – What are you thankful for?

Repent – What are you sorry for?

Ask – What is something you would like to ask God for?

Yield – What is something that you worry about? Give it to God.

The Glorious Mysteries – The Ascension of Jesus into Heaven

Read Philippians 2:5 – 11
Words I Liked

_____
_____
_____
_____
_____
_____
_____

Ascension Holy Card

Master

To ascend means to rise to an important position of power.

_____
_____
_____
_____

St. Paul tells us that "at the name of Jesus every knee should bend." Jesus is meant to be our Master.
What does it mean to say that Jesus is our Master?

Write one thing you love about Jesus.

Write one reason why you are glad you came here.

What is one thing you can thank Jesus for today?

Thank You, Jesus.

What is one thing you would like to say to Jesus today?

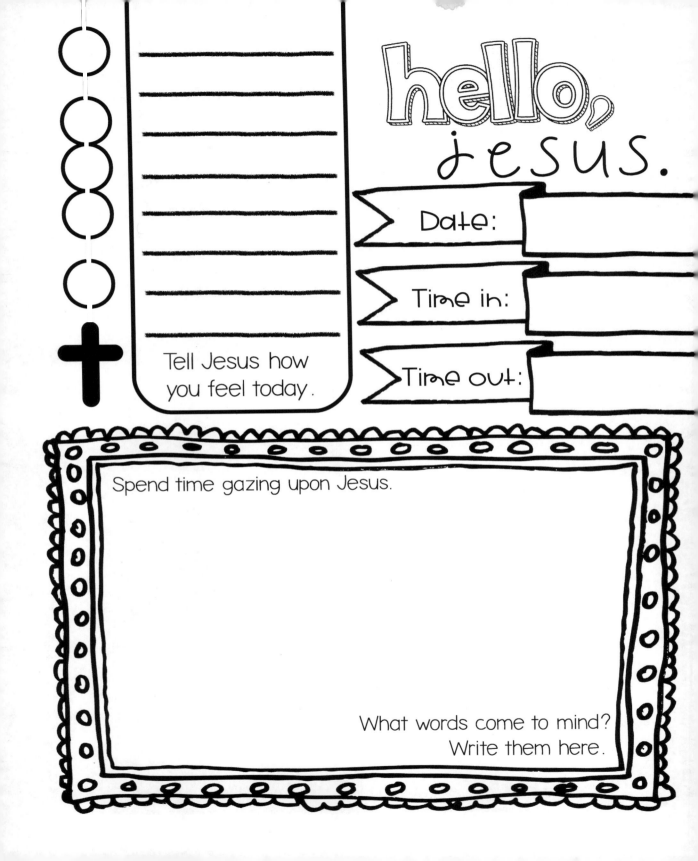

Each letter of the word P.R.A.Y. stands for a different kind of prayer. Use the boxes below to pray each kind of prayer.

Praise – What are you thankful for?

Repent – What are you sorry for?

Ask – What is something you would like to ask God for?

Yield – What is something that you worry about? Give it to God.

The Glorious Mysteries – The Coming of the Holy Spirit at Pentecost

Read 1 John 2:1–2
Words I Liked

_____
_____
_____
_____
_____
_____
_____

Pentecost Holy Card

Advocate

An advocate is someone who supports and encourages someone and speaks to others on their behalf. The Holy Spirit is our Advocate, and so is Jesus.

_____
_____
_____
_____

What does it mean to say that Jesus is our Advocate, especially in the Sacrament of Reconciliation?

Write one thing you love about Jesus.

Write one reason why you are glad you came here.

What is one thing you can thank Jesus for today?

Thank You, Jesus.

What is one thing you would like to say to Jesus today?

Each letter of the word P.R.A.Y. stands for a different kind of prayer. Use the boxes below to pray each kind of prayer.

Praise — What are you thankful for?

Repent — What are you sorry for?

Ask — What is something you would like to ask God for?

Yield — What is something that you worry about? Give it to God.

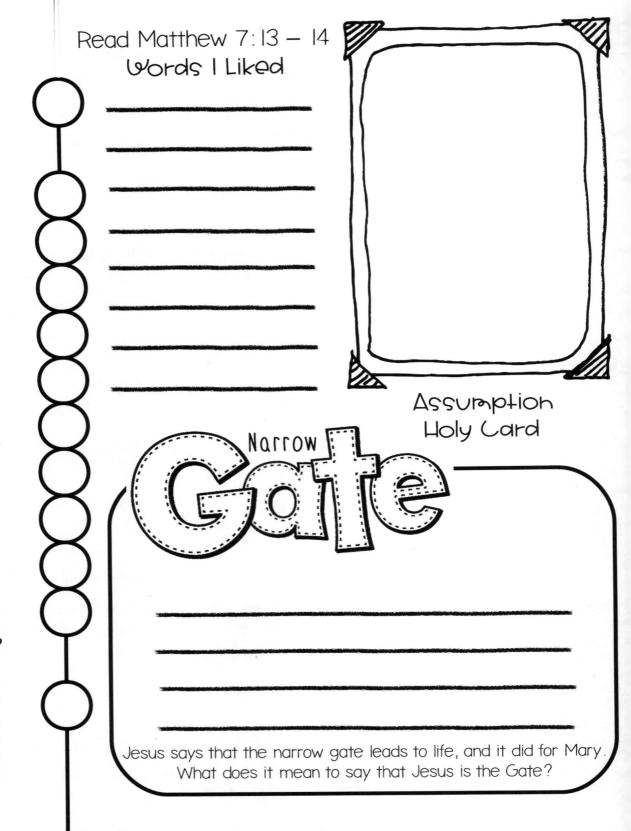

The Glorious Mysteries – The Assumption of the Virgin Mary into Heaven

Read Matthew 7:13 – 14
Words I Liked

Assumption Holy Card

Narrow Gate

Jesus says that the narrow gate leads to life, and it did for Mary. What does it mean to say that Jesus is the Gate?

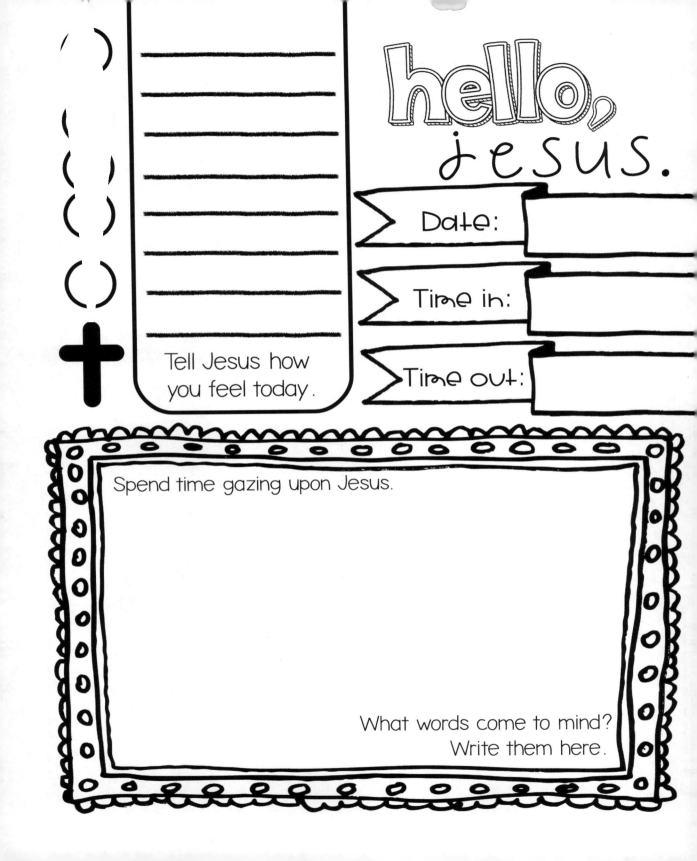

Each letter of the word P.R.A.Y. stands for a different kind of prayer. Use the boxes below to pray each kind of prayer.

 Praise – What are you thankful for?

 Repent – What are you sorry for?

 Ask – What is something you would like to ask God for?

 Yield – What is something that you worry about? Give it to God.

The Glorious Mysteries – The Crowning of Mary as Queen of Heaven and Earth

Read Hebrews 12:1 – 2
Words I Liked
_____
_____
_____
_____
_____
_____
_____

Queen of Heaven Holy Card

Leader and Perfecter
_____
_____
_____

Just like Mary, we also have a choice to make when God asks us to do something. What does it mean to say that Jesus is the Leader and Perfecter of our faith?

Write one thing you love about Jesus.

Write one reason why you are glad you came here.

What is one thing you can thank Jesus for today?

Thank You, Jesus.

What is one thing you would like to say to Jesus today?

Appendix

How to Pray the Rosary

Rosary Prayers

Mysteries of the Holy Rosary

The Books of the Bible

Reconciliation Record

How to Pray the Rosary

1. Begin with the Sign of the Cross.

2. While holding the crucifix, recite the Apostle's Creed.

3. On the first bead, pray an Our Father.

4. Pray a Hail Mary on the next three beads.

5. Finish with a Glory Be.

6. Announce the mystery that you will be focusing on.

7. Pray an Our Father.

8. Pray a Hail Mary on the next ten beads, while meditating on the assigned mystery.

9. Finish with a Glory Be.

10. Repeat steps 6 to 9 until you have completed all five sets of beads.

11. Finish with a Hail, Holy Queen, and then make the Sign of the Cross.

Rosary Prayers

Apostle's Creed

I believe in God,
the Father Almighty,
Creator of heaven and earth,
and in Jesus Christ, His only Son, our Lord,
who was conceived by the Holy Spirit,
born of the Virgin Mary,
suffered under Pontius Pilate,
was crucified, died and was buried;
he descended into hell;
on the third day He rose again from the dead;
he ascended into heaven,
and is seated at the right hand of God the Father Almighty;
from there he will come to judge the living and the dead.
I believe in the Holy Spirit,
the Holy catholic Church,
the communion of saints,
the forgiveness of sins,
the resurrection of the body,
and life everlasting.

Amen.

Rosary Prayers

Our Father

Our Father,
Who art in heaven,
hallowed be thy name;
thy kingdom come;
thy will be done
on earth as it is in heaven.
Give us this day our daily bread;
and forgive us our trespasses
as we forgive those who trespass against us;
and lead us not into temptation,
but deliver us from evil.

Amen.

Hail Mary

Hail Mary, full of grace,
the Lord is with you.
Blessed are you among women,
and blessed is the fruit of
your womb, Jesus.
Holy Mary, Mother of God,
pray for us sinners,
now and at the hour of
our death.

Amen.

Glory Be

Glory be to the Father,
and to the Son,
and to the Holy Spirit.
As it was in the beginning,
is now,
and ever shall be,
world without end.

Amen.

Rosary Prayers
Hail, Holy Queen

Hail, Holy Queen, Mother of Mercy, our life, our sweetness and our hope. To you do we cry, poor banished children of Eve. To you do we send up our sighs, mourning, and weeping in this valley of tears. Turn then, O most gracious advocate, your eyes of mercy toward us, and after this, our exile, show unto us the blessed fruit of your womb, Jesus. O clement! O loving! O sweet Virgin Mary! Pray for us, O Holy Mother of God, that we may be made worthy of the promises of Christ.

Amen.

Mysteries of the Holy Rosary

The Joyful Mysteries

①. The Annunciation of Gabriel to the Virgin Mary — An angel named Gabriel visits Mary and tells her that she has been chosen to be the Mother of Jesus. Mary accepts God's will, and conceives Jesus through the power of the Holy Spirit.

②. The Visitation of the Virgin Mary to Elizabeth — The angel also tells Mary that her cousin, Elizabeth, is pregnant with John the Baptist. Mary goes to visit her, and John the Baptist leaps for joy in Elizabeth's womb!

③. The Birth of Jesus — Jesus is born in Bethlehem, which means, "House of Bread".

④. The Presentation of Jesus in the Temple — Mary and Joseph brought Jesus to the Jewish Temple to present him to God.

⑤. The Finding of the Child Jesus at the Temple — When Jesus is 12, he and his parents visit the Temple for Passover. Jesus is left behind there, and stays in the Temple, talking with the teachers there. Everyone is amazed by his understanding.

Mysteries of the Holy Rosary

The Luminous Mysteries

①. The Baptism of Jesus in the Jordon River – John the Baptist baptizes Jesus in the Jordan River. Jesus models for us the need for baptism, and purifies the waters for us through his baptism.

②. The Wedding Feast at Cana – Mary asks Jesus to help the wedding couple, who have run out of wine for the guests attending their wedding party. Jesus turns large jugs of water into fine wine. This was his first public miracle.

③. The Proclamation of the Kingdom of Heaven – Jesus tells the people the Good News, calling on them to repent of their sins and believe in him.

④. The Transfiguration of Jesus – Jesus, Peter, James, and John go up a high mountain, and Jesus begins to shine with light, showing the disciples his glory. Moses and Elijah appear as well.

⑤. The Institution of the Eucharist at the Last Supper – On Holy Thursday, Jesus changes wine and bread into his Body and Blood for the first time.

Mysteries of the Holy Rosary

The Sorrowful Mysteries

①. The Agony of Jesus in the Garden – Jesus prays alone in a garden the night before he dies. He surrenders to the will of the Father and prepares himself for the Crucifixion.

②. Jesus is Scourged at the Pillar – The soldiers whip and beat Jesus. He endures this suffering for our sake.

③. Jesus is Crowned with Thorns – The soldiers mock Jesus by putting a crown of thorns on his head and a reed in his hand. Then they pretend to bow to him in worship, but really they are mocking him.

④. Jesus Carries the Cross to Calvary – Jesus carries his own cross to the place where he will be crucified. Although he falls under the weight of it, he continues on, knowing that his death is the will of the Father.

⑤. The Crucifixion of Jesus – The soldiers nail Jesus to the cross. Jesus dies, and is buried.

Mysteries of the Holy Rosary

The Glorious Mysteries

①. The Resurrection of Jesus — After three days, Jesus rises from the dead, and appears to many people.

②. The Ascension of Jesus — 40 days after his resurrection, Jesus ascends into Heaven.

③. The Coming of the Holy Spirit at Pentacost — Mary and the Apostles are praying in the Upper Room when the Holy Spirit descends upon them like tongues of fire. Many people are converted to the Church that day after hearing the preaching of St. Peter.

④. The Assumption of the Virgin Mary into Heaven — At the end of Mary's life, God takes her to Heaven, body and soul.

⑤. The Crowning of Mary as Queen of Heaven and Earth — Mary is crowned as Queen of Heaven and Earth. We can ask her to pray on our behalf.

The Books of the Bible

You can use this list to help you look up the passages listed in your adoration journal.

Old Testament

Genesis	Proverbs
Exodus	Ecclesiastes
Leviticus	The Song of Solomon
Numbers	The Wisdom of Solomon
Deuteronomy	Sirach (Ecclesiasticus)
Joshua	Isaiah
Judges	Jeremiah
Ruth	Lamentations
I Samuel	Baruch
II Samuel	Ezekiel
I Kings	Daniel
II Kings	Hosea
I Chronicles	Joel
II Chronicles	Amos
Ezra	Obadiah
Nehemiah	Jonah
Tobit	Micah
Judith	Nahum
Esther	Habakkuk
I Maccabees	Zephaniah
II Maccabees	Haggai
Job	Zechariah
Psalms	Malachi

The Books of the Bible

You can use this list to help you look up the passages listed in your adoration journal.

New Testament

Matthew
Mark
Luke
John
Acts
Romans
I Corinthians
II Corinthians
Galatians
Ephesians
Philippians
Colossians
I Thessalonians
II Thessalonians

I Timothy
II Timothy
Titus
Philemon
Hebrews
James
I Peter
II Peter
I John
II John
III John
Jude
Revelation

Reconciliation Record

1. _____
2. _____
3. _____
4. _____
5. _____
6. _____
7. _____
8. _____
9. _____
10. _____
11. _____
12. _____

Made in the USA
Lexington, KY
28 September 2018